S. HRG. 108–520

DATABASE SECURITY: FINDING OUT WHEN YOUR INFORMATION HAS BEEN COMPROMISED

HEARING

BEFORE THE

SUBCOMMITTEE ON TERRORISM, TECHNOLOGY AND HOMELAND SECURITY

OF THE

COMMITTEE ON THE JUDICIARY

UNITED STATES SENATE

ONE HUNDRED EIGHTH CONGRESS

FIRST SESSION

NOVEMBER 4, 2003

Serial No. J–108–52

Printed for the use of the Committee on the Judiciary

U.S. GOVERNMENT PRINTING OFFICE

94–638 PDF WASHINGTON : 2004

For sale by the Superintendent of Documents, U.S. Government Printing Office
Internet: bookstore.gpo.gov Phone: toll free (866) 512–1800; DC area (202) 512–1800
Fax: (202) 512–2250 Mail: Stop SSOP, Washington, DC 20402–0001

COMMITTEE ON THE JUDICIARY

ORRIN G. HATCH, Utah, *Chairman*

CHARLES E. GRASSLEY, Iowa
ARLEN SPECTER, Pennsylvania
JON KYL, Arizona
MIKE DEWINE, Ohio
JEFF SESSIONS, Alabama
LINDSEY O. GRAHAM, South Carolina
LARRY E. CRAIG, Idaho
SAXBY CHAMBLISS, Georgia
JOHN CORNYN, Texas

PATRICK J. LEAHY, Vermont
EDWARD M. KENNEDY, Massachusetts
JOSEPH R. BIDEN, JR., Delaware
HERBERT KOHL, Wisconsin
DIANNE FEINSTEIN, California
RUSSELL D. FEINGOLD, Wisconsin
CHARLES E. SCHUMER, New York
RICHARD J. DURBIN, Illinois
JOHN EDWARDS, North Carolina

BRUCE ARTIM, *Chief Counsel and Staff Director*
BRUCE A. COHEN, *Democratic Chief Counsel and Staff Director*

SUBCOMMITTEE ON TERRORISM, TECHNOLOGY AND HOMELAND SECURITY

JON KYL, Arizona, *Chairman*

ORRIN G. HATCH, Utah
ARLEN SPECTER, Pennsylvania
MIKE DEWINE, Ohio
JEFF SESSIONS, Alabama
SAXBY CHAMBLISS, Georgia

DIANNE FEINSTEIN, California
EDWARD M. KENNEDY, Massachusetts
JOSEPH R. BIDEN, JR., Delaware
HERBERT KOHL, Wisconsin
JOHN EDWARDS, North Carolina

STEPHEN HIGGINS, *Majority Chief Counsel*
DAVID HANTMAN, *Democratic Chief Counsel*

CONTENTS

STATEMENTS OF COMMITTEE MEMBERS

WITNESSES

QUESTIONS AND ANSWERS

SUBMISSIONS FOR THE RECORD

DATABASE SECURITY: FINDING OUT WHEN YOUR INFORMATION HAS BEEN COMPROMISED

TUESDAY, NOVEMBER 4, 2003

UNITED STATES SENATE,
SUBCOMMITTEE ON TERRORISM, TECHNOLOGY AND HOMELAND SECURITY, COMMITTEE ON THE JUDICIARY,
Washington, DC.

The Subcommittee met, pursuant to notice, at 10:06 a.m., in Room SD–226, Dirksen Senate Office Building, Hon. Jon Kyl, Chairman of the Subcommittee, presiding.

Present: Senators Kyl, Feinstein, and Schumer.

OPENINGS STATEMENT OF HON. JON KYL, A U.S. SENATOR FROM THE STATE OF ARIZONA

Chairman KYL. Good morning. This hearing of the Judiciary Committee Subcommittee on Terrorism, Technology and Homeland Security will come to order.

We have been holding a series of hearings that deal with the nature of terrorism in order to help us better understand how we can combat terrorism. Today, we are going to take time out from that series, and yet the subject with which we deal, like almost everything else that this Subcommittee deals with, also has implications with respect to terrorism.

When we see stories about the theft of a Social Security number, perhaps, by a hacker, or a driver's license or financial information, we understand that this can have many ramifications. It can not only, of course, affect terrorism, as I noted, but can be financially devastating for the people involved, the victims. A criminal can use this information to cause great financial harm.

Senator Feinstein has introduced a bill, S. 1350, the Notification of Risk to Personal Data Act, which addresses the duty of a business maintaining a computerized database with customer-sensitive personal information and has provisions regarding informing customers of a hacking incident that would compromise the personal financial data. Under the bill, notice would be triggered if the hacker obtained access to a customer's Social Security number, driver's license number, or a bank account, debit, or credit card number and the notice would be provided in writing or through e-mail or by some substitute notice.

The notice includes notice by e-mail, the posting of notice on the company or agency website, or notification of major media, and it is triggered if the business can demonstrate that the cost of providing direct notice would be onerous, and there are specific provisions in the bill that relate to that.

Finally, under the bill, the Federal Trade Commission is empowered to fine entities if the violation persists. State Attorneys General could enforce the statute and inconsistent State laws would be preempted, but California's legislation on this subject would be grandfathered in.

Today, the Committee will hear from three expert witnesses. The first is from my home State of Arizona. He is no stranger here to Washington, D.C., but he is involved in very successful ventures today in Arizona. David McIntyre is the President and CEO of TriWest Healthcare Alliance. Mr. McIntyre has a distinguished career in both health care policy and operations. Earlier this year, he guided TriWest in its successful bid for the Defense Department's new West Region, serving military members, retirees, and their families in 21 Western States, including our Ranking Member's State of California, a total of 2.6 million beneficiaries in all.

He will testify about the December 2002 break-in at its Phoenix, Arizona, offices, where thieves broke into a management suite and stole laptop computers and computer hard drives containing the names, address, telephone numbers, birthdates, and Social Security numbers of 562,000 military service members, dependents, and retirees. The thieves also stole medical claims records from people on active duty in the Persian Gulf.

The potential harm to a group obviously this large, particularly to those who wear the uniform of the country, is, of course, staggering. And yet, to date, not a single individual has suffered identity theft as a result of the crime against TriWest. Mr. McIntyre, we look forward to your description of those events and how your company responded to such a major information theft.

Mark MacCarthy, the Senior Vice President of Public Policy for Visa, will testify about the steps that Visa takes to avoid database security breaches and how Visa notifies its customers of security breaches. He will also comment on Senator Feinstein's legislation, S. 1350.

Evan Hendricks, Editor of Privacy Times, will testify about the rise of database security breaches, the types of information stolen from such databases, the failure to notify consumers of such breaches, and the value of notification.

I would like to note that the record will be kept open for one week for questions as well as additional statements and want to thank Senator Feinstein for her hard work in putting together this hearing. I must say that Senator Feinstein and her staff were the primary people helping to put this hearing together, and it is an illustration of the fact that I don't view my Chairmanship of this Committee as anything more than a Co–Chairmanship with Senator Feinstein when it comes to addressing important issues for the American people. So I thank you, Senator Feinstein, for suggesting that we have this hearing and doing a great deal of the work in putting it together.

STATEMENT OF HON. DIANNE FEINSTEIN, A U.S. SENATOR FROM THE STATE OF CALIFORNIA

Senator FEINSTEIN. But you, Mr. Chairman, were the one who said, yes, let us do the hearing, and that counts for a lot, so thank you very much.

I think you have well described the bill. I think one thing has to be said. I am just looking at a pre-publication version of the Richmond Journal of Law and Technology and there is a footnote in it that is very interesting, and what it says is that according to the Computer Security Institute's 2003 Computer Crime and Security Survey, they polled 376 organizations and each one admitted experiencing a security breach in the past year. Half of them said they didn't do anything, and only a third of them reported it. So of a field, everybody has been hacked into and various personal information has been violated, and yet nothing has happened.

California has passed a law. Other States are looking at passing laws. The problem is, will we have 50 different laws throughout America?

Therefore, what this bill aims to do is provide a national standard, a standard that will make sense, that, in essence, defines what data we consider affected by the bill—Social Security numbers, as you just said, driver's license numbers, credit card numbers, debit card numbers, or financial account numbers.

And then, secondly, there is some—personal data is defined in the bill. It minimizes, we hope, the burdens on companies or agencies because we require that they would have to alert someone in writing or through e-mail, and then there are some exceptions. If the companies have developed their own reasonable notification policies, they have a safe harbor. Encrypted data is exempted, and where it is too expensive or impractical to notify every individual who is harmed, the bill allows entities to send out an alternative form of notice called a substitute notice, and that includes posting notice on a website or notifying major media.

I think we have a good bill. It may take amending, but one of the things I hope we are going to hear today is that a bill of this kind, a national standard, in effect, is really necessary if we are to protect people's privacy. Thank you.

Chairman KYL. Thank you, Senator Feinstein.

Let us go directly to our panel, and let us just go from my left to right, first Mr. McIntyre, Mr. MacCarthy, and then Mr. Hendricks. We will then interrupt—or rather than interrupting you, let each of you make your statement and then we will question you at that time. I think we have a five-minute rule here, so if you can stick to that, fine, but we will take all of your written testimony and put it in the record.

Mr. McIntyre?

STATEMENT OF DAVID J. MCINTYRE, JR., PRESIDENT AND CHIEF EXECUTIVE OFFICER, TRIWEST HEALTHCARE ALLIANCE, PHOENIX, ARIZONA

Mr. MCINTYRE. Mr. Chairman, thank you for your very kind introduction and for your long leadership in the important area of identity theft.

Mr. Chairman, Senator Feinstein, thank you for the invitation to appear before you today to discuss an important topic in the legislation before you that would require organizations that suffer the loss of consumer data to disclose that loss to their customers so that they can take timely and meaningful steps to protect themselves from becoming the victims of identity theft. I am particularly honored to be before you today given your leadership in the effort to combat identity theft.

My name is Dave McIntyre. As the Chairman said, I am President and CEO of TriWest Healthcare Alliance. As Chairman Kyl stated, in mid–December, our company was the victim of a physical theft of data. Thieves broke into our offices and stole the hard drives out of our server. We were the third such crime to occur in the State of Arizona in a period of 6 months. Prior to that, there had been a bank that had been broken into after hours and the same thing had occurred.

On our databases were 562,000 individuals' names, addresses, Social Security numbers, birthdates, and other personal information. Thus, it placed those individuals, many of whom wear the uniform of the United States and are serving today in Iraq, in harm's way, in my opinion.

Health care professionals talk about the golden hour when they refer to the window of time in which a heart attack victim must receive medical attention in order to assure the high odds of survival followed by a reasonable quality of life. What I quickly discovered is that there is a golden hour when it comes to aiding consumers in protecting themselves against identity theft.

I was told by industry experts that the most effective measures we could take in our case was to contact within several weeks all of our customers whose personal information was contained in the database to inform them of the theft and assist them in contacting the credit bureaus so that they could place fraud flags on their credit files.

It was this golden hour philosophy that guided our work and that of the Department of Defense and my colleagues in that Department in the days and weeks that followed the theft, which ran, obviously, right through the holiday period. Specifically, we employed a comprehensive and integrated three-prong communication strategy.

First, given the holidays and the need to reach people regardless of where they happened to be, we contacted the media to aid their assistance in broadcasting nationwide the theft and stress the need for individuals to contact us and take action to protect themselves.

Second, given the mobile nature of our customer base, we worked through the military commands worldwide to disseminate information to every installation in the military.

Third, we sent a personal letter to every customer affected by the theft. We just sent out our fourth letter of such kind, advising people of the theft, updating them on it now, and telling them that they needed to add a fraud flag and then keep it updated so that they did not fall prey to whatever the thieves might have had in mind.

By the middle of January, our plan was fully executed, and I believe that the golden hour allowed those individuals to be protected, and I have been told by authorities that not one individual in that database has been confirmed as being a victim of identity theft.

Based on what I have come to learn about the fastest rising crime in America, identity theft, of which no American consumer is immune, I believe that there are three steps that Congress should take to come to the aid of consumers.

First and perhaps most important is to require organizations that are the victims of the theft of their customers' personal information to take swift and effective action to inform the customers of the theft and what measures they can take to protect themselves. I understand personally the difficulty, the cost, and the awkward nature of such disclosure, but to do anything less, in my opinion, is both wrong and indefensible. After all, it is not our organization's information. It is the information of the people who we serve and they have entrusted it to us so that we can serve their needs.

It is for this reason that I appreciate Senator Feinstein's long work in this area and that of the Chairman. I believe that the constructive solutions of S. 1350 are something that need to be enacted, now that we know the risks of this and what the pattern of practice needs to look like.

The second leg of the stool is that I believe that we need to standardize how credit card numbers are displayed on receipts, to block out all but the last four numbers so that no one can take information from a credit card receipt and begin spending in another consumer's name. I believe that such provisions are contained in the legislation to reauthorize the Fair Credit Reporting Act, which I understand will be on the Senate floor this morning for Senate consideration and I think it goes a long way in addressing that issue and worthy of support.

And third, I believe that Federal penalties need to be strengthened so it will no longer be the case that someone spends more time cleaning up their credit than the individual who perpetrated the crime.

Mr. Chairman, Senator Feinstein, I congratulate you on your great work in this area as a consumer. I thank you for your focus and I thank you for the opportunity to be here today.

[The prepared statement of Mr. McIntyre appears as a submission for the record.]

Senator FEINSTEIN. Mr. Chairman, may I say one thing?

Chairman KYL. Certainly.

Senator FEINSTEIN. First of all, thank you, Mr. McIntyre. About Mr. MacCarthy and his company, Visa, when we introduced our big identity theft bill, the CEO of Visa joined us at a press conference and, in essence, indicated that Visa was voluntarily truncating all of their credit card numbers so that when you used a Visa card at a restaurant and you signed your receipt, what you got back had only a part—I forget which part, but only a part of the entire—the last four digits of the credit card. I believe that has been in effect for a substantial period of time. So I just wanted to say thank you to Visa. I think they are a very good corporate citizen and I really appreciate it. Thank you.

Chairman KYL. Thank you. Mr. MacCarthy?

STATEMENT OF MARK MACCARTHY, SENIOR VICE PRESIDENT FOR PUBLIC POLICY, VISA U.S.A., INC., WASHINGTON, D.C.

Mr. MACCARTHY. Mr. Chairman, thank you very much for the kind introduction, and Senator Feinstein, thank you for recognizing the work that Visa does in this area. Our CEO, Carl Pascarella, was pleased to come to Washington to help in that announcement.

The policy you describe, which is to black out all but the last four digits, has been in place for new terminals since June of this year, and after a transition period, it will affect all terminals out in the marketplace, and that was in large part in response to your initiative in the area to push legislation that would address this issue at the Federal level.

Thank you for the invitation to talk about the important issue of consumer information security today. As you know, Visa considers information security to be a top priority. We have long recognized that protecting customer information is important to the integrity of our own system. We are implementing a comprehensive cardholder information security plan that applies to all entities that store, process, transmit, or hold Visa cardholder data. All participating entities must comply with a Visa "digital dozen," 12 basic requirements for safeguarding account information.

In addition, the Visa system includes sophisticated neural networks that flag unusual spending patterns for fraud, and these systems block the authorization of transactions where fraud is suspected.

Visa also has a zero liability policy for unauthorized transactions, which means that customers pay nothing at all when the transaction is unauthorized.

Visa also maintains a worldwide database of account numbers that are lost or stolen. All transactions routed through the Visa system are checked against this file.

Visa believes that the appropriate response to a security breach depends on the specific factors of the breach and the tools available to the financial institutions involved and its customers to address the illicit use of customer information. The response must balance the risk of illicit use of the information against the risk that the response itself may lead to customer cost and inconvenience and disruption in the marketplace.

In the context of the Visa payment system, there are many steps that can be taken to control these risks. The steps available to the customer include closing accounts, putting fraud alerts on their credit reports, reviewing credit bureau files, but these steps serve merely as backstops to the far more sophisticated fraud detection systems currently in place in the Visa system. Moreover, closing accounts, fraud alerts, the review of files of credit bureaus, all involve costs and inconveniences for customers, for financial institutions, and for the marketplace as a whole.

Visa strongly supports customer notification whenever unauthorized access to customer information results in a significant recognizable threat that requires customer action. However, for situations that do not indicate that kind of significant risk, customer notification is not necessary.

Visa believes that it is critical that any notification requirements be sufficiently flexible to allow notice to be provided by the account-holding institution, even if the account-holding institution was not the operator of the system where the breach occurred, they were not the cardholder information custodian. For example, this kind of flexibility would allow the account-holding institution to offer a new account at the same time that it advises the customer that the existing account has to be closed.

Visa is pleased to note that the legislation, S. 1350, is responsive to these issues. It establishes a general policy for customer notification in the context of security breaches and it permits the use of alternative notification procedures in the case that includes a security program that is designed to block unauthorized transactions before they are charged to a customer's account, and that is subject to examination by the Federal banking regulators. S. 1350 also provides for the kind of flexibility in delivering required notices that I just referred to.

Finally, Visa is pleased to note that S. 1350 recognizes the importance of establishing consistent procedures for notifying individuals about security breaches and supercedes inconsistent State and local laws.

I appreciate the opportunity to appear before you today. Combatting information security breaches, combatting identity theft will continue to be a top priority for Visa and its member financial institutions and I would be happy to answer any questions you have.

Chairman KYL. I would note, Senator Feinstein, that this is a great panel. They are right to the second on their 5 minutes, so we appreciate that very much. You are very succinct, but you have said it all. Thank you very much.

[The prepared statement of Mr. MacCarthy appears as a submission for the record.]

Chairman KYL. Mr. Hendricks?

STATEMENT OF EVAN HENDRICKS, EDITOR/PUBLISHER, PRIVACY TIMES, CABIN JOHN, MARYLAND

Mr. HENDRICKS. The advantage of having a privacy expert appear before you, this brings a little history. I enjoyed back in the late 1990's working with your staff, Senator Kyl, and your consistent, Mr. Hardle, in getting the first identity theft law passed in this country on a national level and I have thoroughly enjoyed working with Senator Feinstein on the FCRA Amendments, which go to the floor today. We really appreciate your leadership on trying to fight for Americans' right to privacy on that. We don't want—

Senator FEINSTEIN. It is an uphill battle.

Mr. HENDRICKS. Yes, it is an uphill battle and we don't want a consumer protection law to be turned into something that deprives people of hard-fought privacy rights, but whether short-term or long-term, we are confident that you will prevail on that, so thank you.

The issue of notification first came up for me in the early 1990's when it was discovered that information brokers were bribing Social Security Administration employees for wage data. This was a systematic and widespread assault which led to Senate hearings. At that time, the Social Security Administration refused to notify the people who were the victims of those very serious breaches and I started raising the issue then.

What is interesting—the reason I think this bill is a very good starting point and can accomplish a lot of good in setting a national standard here is because it is true to some of the issues of fair information practice principles, which really govern our privacy laws, like the Fair Credit Reporting Act and the Privacy Act.

People think privacy is hiding in the closet or just trying to keep things secret, but how we really define it is how we abide by these principles which include access and correction, transparency, data security, data minimization, and limiting the purposes for which data can be used. And this bill understands, goes right to the heart of sunshine is the best disinfectant. It brings out transparency for the issue of how data is used, and you will see how—one reason Mr. McIntyre was so successful in responding to the crisis they had is they went very public and brought a lot of attention to what was going on. So I think that is why this is a good starting point.

I think one of the reasons it is needed is, as mentioned, identity theft is the fastest growing crime in the United States. There are so many studies out this summer by the FTC, the GAO, the Gartner Group, Privacy in American Business, that says it is far worse than we even expected and that the biggest threat to information security is by authorized insiders using their authorized insiderness to use information for unauthorized purposes. So, therefore, that is a real threat, and more and more information is being collected in databases and we have to have a way of notifying people when things go wrong.

Another problem is that we don't have an organizational culture of privacy and security. We don't see the kind of consciousness that you saw in TriWest and you don't normally see the kind of leadership you saw in Visa on the issues Senator Feinstein mentioned.

Just in the recent Victoria's Secret case, which was prosecuted by New York Attorney General Elliott Spitzer, they found out that you could get access to people's purchases through their website. It was just one of those glitches, but when a customer notified Victoria's Secret about it, they said there were no credit card numbers involved so what is the big deal? And it was only after he went to the media that he was able to get attention, and it was only because Attorney General Spitzer investigated that they were able to get notice to the New Yorkers who were affected by that, and as far as I know, the other people who were affected who weren't New Yorkers did not receive notice. So you see there is going to be an ongoing problem here.

Another thing that is very new that is just coming up this year is the outsourcing of the personal data processing to other countries. We know that—I think the USDA does it with food stamps. The San Francisco Chronicle just did a story October 22 saying that an employee in Pakistan who was doing medical transcription then was not getting paid and so her way of handling that was to threaten to post the medical patient details on the Internet as a way of extorting—getting paid what she was owed. The San Francisco Chronicle is now hot on this story and they are pursuing it.

We reported that the credit bureaus, the big credit bureaus, Equifax outsources to Jamaica and Experion and Trans Union are going to be going to either the Philippines or India or both. These raise serious questions about how will data be protected as it goes across our borders and can Americans feel secure in that. So that is another reason why this bill is so important.

I mentioned that fair information practices are the gold standard for measuring how well are we protecting privacy, and that is why this bill is a good starting point. The other things to consider is whether we should provide in this bill a right of access to people's information. People have this right under the Fair Credit Reporting Act to their credit reports. They have it under the Privacy Act and the Freedom of Information Act for their government records, under HIPAA for their medical records. We need to keep filling the gaps here where people do not have access to their records because the data kept about them says a lot about them and decisions are being made on that data.

I think, for this bill specifically, I think we should consider when notification is not required and it is really not considered a thing where it is too costly to notify people, which I think is a reasonable standard, I think we still have to have a way that if people want to find out what happened or what was the practices and what is their system for notifying, that people have a right to find out and the company has to answer their questions, because we have seen in cases in the past when we know there is a hack, we know there is a problem, but we can't find any more information, and so people are just left in the dark, not knowing what happened.

I think another thing, since we are trying to advance data security, we have the 30-year-old standard from the Privacy Act about how organizations should just take appropriate administrative, technical, and physical safeguards to ensure against anticipated threats that can harm individuals. That standard is also sort of becoming the standard for financial institutions under the Gramm–Leach–Bliley regulations.

I think, finally, enforcement of this bill is left to the FTC and the State Attorney Generals, which have always been the leaders in enforcement in this area, but I still think you need a private right of action for the most egregious cases. We will never be able to build a bureaucracy big enough to enforce a system that is covering the records of 200 million Americans. We don't want trivial or specious lawsuits brought, but we need to give people rights when the organizational behavior is egregious or it has been going on for many years and there is a pattern and practice, and where I think a good standard, a high standard to meet for that is like gross negligence or reckless disregard for people's rights. But we need to give individuals the right to enforce their own rights.

The final thing is the Social Security number. There are bills pending by Senator Feinstein and others that would try and limit the circulation of SSNs in our society and, ultimately, on the creation of a national standard. We think this bill is a good bill to the extent that it creates a floor and says that you cannot have laws that are inconsistent with it. And I don't think you really need to out and out preempt state laws because if, first of all, if you do this law, then States will move on and they won't need to enact laws in the States. They will see that the Congress is taking care of it, which is really why I commend you for getting out in front of this issue. You save a lot of those problems.

Ultimately, though, I am reluctant to say we should shut out States altogether because this is such a fast-moving area and States often come up with some very creative solutions to these fast-moving problems.

Thanks, and I apologize for going over my time.

Chairman KYL. I am sure Senator Feinstein joins me in saying these are all very constructive suggestions and things that we obviously need to look at.

[The prepared statement of Mr. Hendricks appears as a submissions for the record.]

Chairman KYL. The last point that you raised prompts me to just make an observation and raise this question, both with regard to the Social Security legislation and this legislation. There are a large number of databases that are outside of the business field, and that is obviously government of one kind or another. I was just telling Senator Feinstein that the Clerk of the County Court System in Maricopa County, Arizona, talked to me about the large volume of information which they have which is not in a form that would be easily protectable under the standards of this legislation and it would be very good for us, if we are going to devise a new format, to be sure that we include that in government databases, which are also subject to the same degree of hacking or theft that business databases are. If any of you have a comment on that, please make that.

Mr. HENDRICKS. You go first.

Mr. MACCARTHY. I think that it is important to make sure that as we are dealing with this issue, that we are dealing with both hacking and physical theft, and I would say that from my perspective, public institutions are not immune to this problem.

Sir, you are talking about the Maricopa County system. The head of the Arizona State University system and a number of the Boards of Regents, members of the Boards of Regents in Arizona told me recently that our experience was an eye-opener to them, and they took this issue to the regents and started doing a study of the university system in the State. There isn't a week that goes by in the State of Arizona that someone hasn't attempted to hack into either the financial, the grading system, or the personnel systems in that institution.

You know, this is a fast-moving train. What is going to be good enough today isn't going to be good enough a couple of years from now, and I think what you are doing is bringing a lot of necessary attention to this issue. But we do need to have a dialogue about the public institutions, not just the private institutions.

Chairman KYL. Thank you. I also note that we are planning right now a hearing on cyber terrorism for the first—after we return next year. It prompts me to think maybe we should expand that slightly, not just to terrorism, but hacking generally and the kind of things that can occur in the business sector and the public sector with that.

Mr. MACCARTHY. Right.

Chairman KYL. Let me just ask two quick questions of each of you and then turn to Senator Feinstein. We are talking about some kind of a uniform standard, I presume. My question really has to do with the expense to business for that as well as how we can make sure that we achieve the maximum notification for the most efficient cost. Clearly—and this is a point, Mr. Hendricks, that you mentioned—we don't want the obligations here to be so onerous that we defeat our own purpose by making them too expensive and, therefore, have blow-back against our ideas here because of the expense. Mr. MacCarthy?

Mr. MACCARTHY. Mr. Chairman, let me return to the previous question. Our cardholder information security program applies to all entities that touch Visa cardholder information, public or private. So we think any kind of security regime should extend across the board and include all people who hold sensitive data.

On the particular question, we think that the legislation is balanced. It does recognize the significant risk principle where information is provided to customers in the context of a significant risk of harm. We think it provides the flexibility for working out the way that notification could take place. We like its consistent national approach. We think it does—the key elements that need to be in Federal legislation are incorporated in that bill.

Chairman KYL. Thank you.

Mr. HENDRICKS. Yes, and I think this will always be a case-by-case, which is good about your bill, because you leave it to sort of you have to have a reasonableness standard. Let us say in California, all the public employees are hit by some hack. Well, if all those employees get the same newsletter or if you have the e-mail addresses, then it becomes very inexpensive. And, of course, as we move into the electronic environment, communicating and notifying via e-mail is not expensive or burdensome at all. So that is something we have to look forward to.

I think that each case by case, you can get creative ways to try and notify people. But if you have just like a huge population, it is not feasible to have to send notice to like 100 million people, and I don't see the bill ever requiring that.

Mr. MCINTYRE. Sir, I would associate myself with the remarks of my colleagues on the panel.

Chairman KYL. Senator Feinstein?

Senator FEINSTEIN. Thank you very much. Senator Schumer came in on a matter, and I missed part of your statement, Mr. MacCarthy, but I was going to ask you, you testified that a significant recognizable threat is necessary for disclosure. How would you define significant recognizable threat?

Mr. MACCARTHY. I think that may turn out to be a judgment call, depending on the specific facts. It may be useful to explain what happens in the Visa system when there is a breach to give you a sense of the kind of circumstance we are talking about.

Senator FEINSTEIN. Good. That would be helpful.

Mr. MACCARTHY. When there is a breach, the cardholder numbers that are affected are treated as a separate group of account numbers, a portfolio, if you will—

Senator FEINSTEIN. So you immediately know which cardholders are affected?

Mr. MACCARTHY. If the merchant or the processor or the person who had the breach notifies us, then given the cardholder numbers, we know immediately the financial institutions involved and they will know immediately the names of the people involved based on the cardholder number that they have.

Senator FEINSTEIN. Do you do regular reviews to find this?

Mr. MACCARTHY. In the context that I am talking about—

Senator FEINSTEIN. Because a hacker is not going to tell you before they do it.

Mr. MACCARTHY. No, they don't tell you before, but when there is a breach, typically what happens is the entity that holds the cardholder information knows about the breach very shortly after it happens and they inform us directly. It is required under our rules that they tell Visa directly that there has been a breach and provide us with the cardholder numbers. When that happens, we then keep those numbers in a central computer location, treat them as a group. We also notify the financial institutions immediately—

Senator FEINSTEIN. Stop for a minute. You mean if I hold, say, a Visa on Bank of America, the Bank of America would notify you?

Mr. MACCARTHY. For example, a merchant that—not Bank of America, or it could be Bank of America if they are the custodian of information that has had a cardholder breach. But in a typical circumstance, it is a third party, a merchant or a processor, that keeps Visa information on file as part of the transaction that they have had with you.

Senator FEINSTEIN. And explain to me, how does he know?

Mr. MACCARTHY. Well, this is what happens when a breach occurs. The entity that is the custodian of the information typically knows that there has been a breach, sometimes not immediately, but typically they do find out, and when they do find out that there has been a breach, they notify us. They notify the FBI, the Secret Service. They work with law enforcement very, very quickly to see if they can control the consequences of the breach.

Once we get the information, we have the cardholder information, we can look at those accounts and we can tell whether or not there is any unusual pattern of fraud, any types of fraud, any elevated risk to cardholders. And when you notice that there are those patterns of excess fraud, unusual patterns or suspicious patterns, the cardholder's institution and Visa work together to make sure that the cardholder is notified, and in some situations, instead of just notification, the account is terminated and a new card is issued.

Senator FEINSTEIN. Can you just give us an approximate number of breaches that you would have this way in a year?

Mr. MACCARTHY. I can't give you that information at this point. Let me go back and work on that and see if I can get back to you on it.

Senator FEINSTEIN. I mean, is it thousands?

Mr. MACCARTHY. In some circumstances, in single breaches, you could have a large number of cardholders' information that are compromised, and those, as I say, are then put on special watch to make sure that there is no risk of harm to consumers in that kind of context.

And also in that kind of circumstance, if there is unauthorized use of cardholder information, the cardholder himself or herself is not responsible for paying the bill. It is unauthorized use. They have zero liability.

Senator FEINSTEIN. Thank you. Anybody else?

Mr. HENDRICKS. In the case earlier this year, the famous one, which I think was called DPI, it was a credit card processing company, it was known that there were over 10 million credit card numbers were taken in that hack, but there is no evidence that anything was ever done with them.

One of the problems that we had from our side in that is that you couldn't find out which member banks were the ones hit, because under contract, they are not allowed to disclose that. So their contracts did not allow the kind of transparency we needed to assure consumers that they were safe in this thing.

You asked, well, how do you define a significant threat? I think one way you don't want to do is restrict it to simply economic harm or theft of your credit card number and purchases made. What I have seen over the years, and statistics bear me out, what Americans really care about is protection of their reputation and their good name, and that is why you see the complaints to the Federal Trade Commission are overwhelmingly about identity theft, because they don't lose money out of pocket on that, but it directly attacks their reputation and good name, where complaints about Internet scams and other forms of fraud which do involve out-of-pocket losses are down in the eight to ten percent level where identity theft is up in the 42 percent level. So we want to make sure that we define it in a way so we include both economic harm, harm to reputation and good name, and the emotional distress arising from when you know your information is taken and the steps are not being taken to protect it.

Senator FEINSTEIN. Thank you. Thank you.

Mr. McIntyre, do you have any comments on that point?

Mr. MCINTYRE. I think Mr. MacCarthy had a follow-up and then I would be glad to comment.

Senator FEINSTEIN. All right, fine.

Mr. MACCARTHY. Back on the DIP case, Evan is right that there were about ten million cards that were compromised. Some of them were Visa cards, but there were also Master Card, American Express, and Discover cards involved. We put them on a watch on the Visa cards and there is no excess of fraud among those cards. So the harm to consumer isn't present in that kind of circumstance.

We did, however, think that the processor involved hadn't done everything that they could do to keep the information safe. They had not been in compliance with our cardholder information security program and the violation wasn't small, it was egregious. We fined them $500,000.

Senator FEINSTEIN. Wow.

Mr. MACCARTHY. And they are on special watch at this point. They can't sign up any more merchants until they have satisfied us that their procedures in place are adequate.

Senator FEINSTEIN. Good for you.

Mr. MCINTYRE. Senator, I think that the definition around what is significant will be fluid and I think the way your legislation is written provides for reasonable coverage of that definition. From a business point of view, I don't find it to be egregious at all.

The issue with regard to what Mark was talking about on the Visa side, I have been monitoring this issue very closely at a personal level since the middle of December, since I learned a lot more about this topic, and it was ironic, because the day after our theft when we started working on what we were going to do in response to it, I got a call from my Visa card company saying, we wanted to make sure that you were traveling to such-and-such a location and such-and-such a location and such-and-such a location, because I had been in three States in 1 day, and that is not the typical pattern of travel for most people, and I had shopped or eaten in three different places in a day. I think the Visa card companies have done a great job in being able to track that.

Significant to the standard today is going to be different than significant to the standard 2 years from now when we are much more complex in terms of the capability to both see physical theft as well as hacking in this area.

Senator FEINSTEIN. [Presiding.] Very good. Incidentally, Senator Kyl had to leave. He had an urgent appointment, so I would essentially like to do this. I think you have all reviewed the legislation. If you have any other comments on how we might strengthen it or, Mr. MacCarthy, for example, on the safe harbor, if a company has its own procedures that are adequate, that may need some more defining, we would really appreciate it.

Let me ask you if you have any other remarks to make on the subject. If not, I will close the hearing.

Mr. MCINTYRE. The last observation that I would offer, and I know that this has been an area of great focus for you for some time, and that is the use of Social Security numbers. After we suffered the theft in our State, we made a commitment that this was a public affairs area that we are going to remain in for some time because we went so public and it gave us a platform to help other businesses and entities in the State of Arizona.

And one of the things that we did as a spinoff from that was to let the Blue Cross–Blue Shield Association know that having your Social Security number on your insurance card probably isn't a very good idea and that there needs to be some way to begin to pare down those numbers. They are looking at that issue.

You know, when you get into the health care space, everyone sees doctors every year and gets health care experience in the marketplace every year, and oftentimes what they get back is a report from their insurance company through the claims processor. And more often than not, what is contained on those forms is your entire Social Security number.

I reviewed this issue with the Department of Defense, as well, because we used to have an identification number for military personnel. Prior to that, it was Social Security numbers. Now we are at a Social Security number again. And the question was, what do we do to protect the military personnel from the misuse of their identity through payroll acquisition or whatever?

And in looking at that, it seems to me that the same principle could be applied as the one that is being applied on the credit card side, which is to "X" out all but the last four numbers. We have proposed that to the DOD on the health care side and we are in the process of working that through.

Senator FEINSTEIN. On the Social Security number?

Mr. MCINTYRE. That is correct, in addition to the credit cards. So you could apply the same concept there. It is easy to build software from a practical operations perspective to put in place to scrub the numbers as they go through. But to upend an entire system and go to a new identification number is something that is fraught with all kinds of other issues. And even then, I would say you need to truncate those numbers except for all but very critical use.

So you are on the right issue. This is a very, very important area and I think that you have got your arms wrapped around the right legs of the stool and look forward to supporting you as you move forward.

Senator FEINSTEIN. Thank you. One thing that you might be able to help with is Senator Gregg and I have had a Social Security number bill—

Mr. MCINTYRE. Yes, ma'am.

Senator FEINSTEIN. —to prevent its commercialization and selling it and that kind of thing. We have had a devil of a time getting it out of the Finance Committee, where it seems to be residing, and we don't want it to find its burial place there. So anything you could do to weigh in on that, and perhaps take a look at the bill and see if you have any concerns about it—

Mr. MCINTYRE. We would be glad to do that.

Senator FEINSTEIN. We would appreciate that very much.

Mr. MCINTYRE. Yes, Senator, and we look forward to serving the constituents in your good State.

Senator FEINSTEIN. Thank you. Thank you very much. And the same would go for you, Mr. Hendricks, and even Mr. MacCarthy, if you would like.

Let me thank you for your testimony today. I think it has been very useful. I think this is a hard area to negotiate in and to legislate in because the technology moves so fast, it is hard to keep up with it. But I really appreciate your testimony and I appreciate your support of the bill. So thank you very much, and the hearing is adjourned.

[Whereupon, at 10:50 a.m., the Subcommittee was adjourned.]

[Questions and answers and submissions for the record follow.]

PRIVACY TIMES

EDITOR: EVAN HENDRICKS

Faxed To: Barr Hueffner 202 224 9102
In Re: Response To Sen. Feinstein's Question on Private Right of Action

Dear Senator Feinstein:

A private right of action is both vital and fundamental if a privacy law is to be effective. This is because "privacy" is *for* individuals, and because for a law to be effective, it must be enforceable. When it comes to enforcing privacy-Fair Information Practices laws, Federal agencies have a spotty history at best. (See, for example, my new book, "Credit Scores and Credit Reports: How The System Really Works, What You Can Do [Privacy Times, 2004], Chapters 10, & 21-22.)

Individuals must be empowered to enforce their own rights. Hence, the private right of action is essential. A privacy law without a private right of action is a hollow, "paper tiger," which can give consumers a false sense of security.

An example of this is the Gramm-Leach-Bliely Act, which fails to incorporate traditional principles of Fair Information Practices and does not include a private right of action. Instead, GLB totally relies on notice, which by itself, is never enough.

Evan Hendricks
Editor/Publisher
Privacy Times (24th Year)
www.privacytimes.com

Author
Credit Scores and Credit Reports: How The System Really Works, What You Can Do
www.CreditScoresandCreditReports.com

Privacy Times P.O. Box 302 Cabin John, MD 20818
(301) 229 7002 (301) 229 8011 [fax] evan@privacytimes.com

Joe

MARK MACCARTHY
Senior Vice President
Public Policy

VISA
WORLDWIDE PARTNER

December 17, 2003

By U.S. Mail
Via E-Mail

The Honorable Jon Kyl
Subcommittee on Terrorism,
Technology and Homeland Security
Senate Committee on the Judiciary
SD-224 Dirksen Senate Office Building
Washington, DC 20510-6275
Attention: Barr Huefner

Re: Private Cause of Action Inquiry

Dear Mr. Chairman:

Thank you for the opportunity to respond to Senator Feinstein's inquiry regarding the addition of a private cause of action to S. 1350, the "Notification of Risk to Personal Data Act" (S. 1350).

In the inquiry, Senator Feinstein asked for Visa's views as to whether a private cause of action should be added to S. 1350. While Visa strongly supports the idea of national standards for consumer notification and the protection of consumer data contained within electronic databases, Visa does not support the addition of a private cause of action to S. 1350.

Visa recognizes that S. 1350 is concerned with both consumer privacy and the risk of consumer identity theft. However, losses associated with consumer identity theft are typically borne by the individual financial institutions that are defrauded. The potential harms suffered by consumers from information security breaches are largely non-monetary and difficult to value. In addition, the technical aspects of information security breaches make it a difficult task for disparate courts to assess the relative culpability of the parties involved and to render effective and consistent decisions. In this context, Visa believes that the addition of a private cause of action to S. 1350 will lead to unwarranted lawsuits and unpredictable judicial decisions.

In contrast, the bank regulatory agencies have at their disposal comprehensive and reliable examination and enforcement powers. Bank regulatory agencies can use information technology examinations, expert examiners, and peer group comparisons to ensure appropriate

VISA U.S.A. INC.
1300 Connecticut Avenue, NW
Suite 900
Washington, DC 20036
U.S.A.

The Honorable Jon Kyl
December 17, 2003
Page Two

compliance with S. 1350. The bank regulatory agencies also have the ability to issue cease and desist orders for banking institutions that are in violation of S. 1350, and the ability to levy substantial monetary fines of up to one million dollars per day under the Federal Deposit Insurance Act.

Moreover, the ability of bank regulatory agencies to examine companies providing services to banks will enable the agencies to require banking institutions to police their servicing companies for S. 1350 compliance. Further, companies providing services to banks and other companies outside of the banking industry would be subject to the jurisdiction of the Federal Trade Commission to enforce compliance, including the assessment of specified fines.

For these reasons, Visa believes that the federal regulatory agencies will be the most appropriate enforcement vehicles for the provisions of S. 1350 without the addition of a private cause of action. I would be happy to answer any additional questions that you may have.

Best regards,

Mark MacCarthy

TRIWEST
HEALTHCARE ALLIANCE®

December 12, 2003

The Honorable Jon Kyl
Chairman, Subcommittee on Terrorism, Technology & Homeland Security
730 Hart Senate Office Building
Washington, DC 20510-0304

Dear ~~Senator Kyl~~ Jon:

Thank you for the opportunity to testify before your Subcommittee on November 4, and for the opportunity to follow-up in response to your additional question. With regard to the issue of a private cause of action, particularly as it relates to the California State example, I believe it might be useful to review the experience of TriWest Healthcare Alliance and the theft of information pertaining to the 560,000 individuals in the stolen data base. At the outset, let me state that our experience has clearly shown that individuals have a very real expectation that the personal information they entrust to an organization should be treated with the greatest care. And in the event of an inadvertent breach in that information's security, I believe consumers have an absolute right to be informed of the risk to themselves and their identity. This right does suggest government action to ensure an effective process of informing consumers.

At the same time, consumers in this country are not likely to receive a benefit equal to the potential economic harm if the courts become clogged with the massive number of lawsuits that could result from a direct legal response to identity theft. As we've seen in the area of medical liability, it is quite possible that excessive legal action could result in incalculable cost to the public without producing corresponding benefit to consumers. In my view, it is irresponsible public policy to purport to provide consumer protection by pursuing a "pound of flesh" response after crimes have been committed. Instead, the government has a responsibility to help ensure the maximum protection against identity theft by encouraging and requiring adequate notification to individuals impacted by information theft before their identities are stolen.

Your question indicated that the State did not learn of the breach for a month and "did not report the breach to the affected employees for another two weeks." In our case, the theft occurred sometime on a Saturday, was discovered the following Monday morning, but it took nearly a week to determine the extent of the information stolen.

15451 North 28th Ave. ★ Phoenix, Arizona 85053
Phone: (602) 564-2000 ★ Fax: (602) 564-2049 ★ http://www.triwest.com

December 12, 2003
Page 2

At that point, we undertook an extraordinary effort to notify every individual who had information on the stolen hard drives - including an aggressive media campaign, letters to each individual potentially at risk, and, with the assistance of the Defense Department, communication to military commanders literally around the world. This effort required an investment of millions of dollars and employee time, and we've continued to meet our commitment to inform these individuals, at further expense, every quarter.

As a result of this experience, we've been devoted to ensuring that each potentially threatened individual had all the information necessary to protect their credit and their identity. This has included both a broad public information campaign as well as direct communication through letters, a dedicated website and working through the military communication network. Likewise, since the first days of our information theft, we have coordinated closely with the credit bureaus. These organizations have gone to great lengths over the past year to ensure that their processes are simpler and more efficient in order to minimize any further difficulty for individuals once they've learned their information has been compromised.

Rather than create a whole new arena for litigation, involving potentially millions of victims who may or may not suffer actual harm, I encourage the Committee to continue on its present course to ensure the greatest possible efforts are made to prevent this terribly invasive and disruptive crime.

Sincerely,

David J. McIntyre, Jr.
President and CEO

cc: Senator Dianne Feinstein

SUBMISSIONS FOR THE RECORD

News from . . .

Senator Dianne Feinstein

of California

FOR IMMEDIATE RELEASE:
Tuesday, November 4, 2003

Contact: Howard Gantman
or Scott Gerber 202/224-9629
http://feinstein.senate.gov/

Statement of Senator Feinstein on Legislation to Ensure Individuals are Notified when Personal Information is Stolen from Databases

Washington, DC *– At a hearing of the Senate Judiciary Subcommittee on Terrorism, Technology, and Homeland Security, Senator Dianne Feinstein (D-Calif.) today called on her colleagues to approve legislation which she sponsored that would require businesses or government agencies to notify individuals if a database has been broken into and personal data has been compromised, including Social Security numbers, driver's licenses and credit cards.*

The following is the prepared text of Senator Feinstein's statement:

"Good morning. I am delighted that we are having this hearing today to discuss the ever-growing problem of identity theft and the measures that are needed to protect consumers in this country from this terrible crime which plagued nearly one million Americans last year. Over the last several years, identity theft ranks as the leading consumer fraud complaint filed with the Federal Trade Commission.

The type of protection we are here to discuss is the rights of consumers to be notified if their personal information has been stolen from a database run by the government or by any private company.

I want to thank my colleague and friend Senator Kyl for chairing this hearing so that we can discuss the scope of the problem and how to solve it.

This problem requires our attention because all Americans are consumers. We are all potential victims of the crime of identity theft. Because the problem has a national scope, in June of this year, I introduced the Notification of Risk to Personal Data Act. This legislation requires the government or private entities to notify individuals when their most sensitive personal information is stolen from a government or corporate database.

The personal information includes Social Security numbers, driver's license numbers, credit card numbers, debit card numbers, or financial account numbers.

In most cases, if authorities know that someone is a victim of a crime, the victim is notified. But that isn't the case if an individual's most sensitive personal information is stolen from an electronic database.

I strongly believe individuals have a right to be notified when their most sensitive information is compromised – because it is truly their information. And they have the right to decide what actions they want to take once a breach has been discovered.

Unfortunately, data breaches are becoming all too common and current law does not require notification to consumers when these breaches occur. Consider the following incidents which have compromised the records of hundreds of thousands of Americans.

- In August of this year, Daniel Baas was arrested and charged by federal prosecutors in Ohio with breaking into the computer databases of a company called Axiom Corporation which analyzes consumer databases for a variety of companies, including several Fortune 500 firms and downloading sensitive information about some of its clients' customers. The affidavit which was filed by law enforcement stated that Baas claimed he had access to private phone databases from Cincinnati Bell, AT&T Mobile, Sprint PCS and Nestle. This breach has caused Axiom about $1.5 million in damage.

- In February 2003, a hacker gained access to ten million Visa, MasterCard, American Express Card and Discover Card numbers from the databases of a credit processor, DPI Merchant services of Omaha, Nebraska. Company officials maintained that the intruder did not obtain any personal information for these card numbers such as the account holder's name, address, telephone number or Social Security number. However, at least one bank canceled and replaced 8,800 cards when it found out about the security breach.

- On April 5, 2002, a hacker broke into the electronic records of the Steven P. Teale Data Center, the payroll facility for California state employees. The hacker compromised files containing the first initials, middle initials, and last names, Social Security numbers, and payroll deduction information of approximately 265,000 people.

- On December 14th, 2002, TriWest Health Care Alliance, a company that provides health care coverage for military personnel and their families, was burglarized. Personal information including names, addresses and Social Security numbers of over 500,000 military service members, dependents and retirees were stolen from the company's computer databases. I understand that Mr. McIntyre, the President and CEO of TriWest is here today to talk about what happened in his company, the steps that his company took to notify their beneficiaries, and steps that his company has taken since this breach to try and avoid these problems in the future.

These are just some examples of the types of breaches that are occurring today and states are taking action. My own state of California has a state notification law which requires companies or agencies to tell individuals of the misappropriation of their personal data. But this is a national problem and requires a national solution.

Let me take a moment to describe the legislation I introduced this past June:

The legislation requires a business or government entity to notify an individual when there is a reasonable basis to conclude that a hacker or other criminal has obtained unencrypted personal data maintained by the entity.

Personal data is defined by the bill as an individual's Social Security number, State identification number, driver's license number, financial account number, credit card number, or credit card number.

The legislation's notification scheme minimizes the burdens on companies or agencies that must report a data breach.

In general, notice would have to be provided to each person whose data was compromised in writing or through e-mail. But there are important exceptions.

First, companies that have developed their own reasonable notification policies are given a safe harbor under the bill and are exempted from its notification requirements.

Second, encrypted data is exempted.

Third, where it is too expensive or impractical (e.g, contact address information is incomplete) to notify every individual who is harmed, the bill allows entities to send out an alternative form of notice called "substitute notice." Substitute notice includes posting notice on a website or notifying major media.

The bill has a tough, but fair enforcement regime. Entities that fail to comply with the bill will be subject to fines by the Federal Trade Commission of $5,000 per violation or up to $25,000 per day while the violation persists. State Attorneys General can also file suit to enforce the statute.

Additionally, the bill would allow California's new law to remain in effect, but preempt conflicting state laws. It is not fair to put companies in a situation that forces them to comply with database notification laws of 50 different states.

I look forward to working with my colleagues to pass this important legislation. This bill will give all Americans more control and confidence about the safety of their personal information. Americans will have the security of knowing that should a breach occur, they will be notified and be able to take protective action. All Americans deserve that sense of security.

If individuals are informed of the theft of their Social Security numbers or other sensitive information, they can take immediate preventative action.

- They can place a fraud alert on their credit report to prevent crooks from obtaining credit cards in their name;
- They can monitor their credit reports to see if unauthorized activity has occurred;
- They can cancel any affected financial or consumer or utility accounts;
- They can change their phone numbers if necessary;

Prompt notification will also help combat the growing scourge of identity theft. According to the Identity Theft Resources Center, a typical identity theft victim takes six to 12 months to discover that a fraud has been perpetuated against them.

I look forward to hearing the testimony today so that we can get a fuller picture of the problem of database security breaches and the preventative steps companies are taking to address these problems and to notify individuals when these breaches arise."

A summary of the bill is attached.

The *"Notification of Risk to Personal Data Act"* would set a much needed national standard for notification of consumers when a database breach occurs. Specifically, the legislation would:

- Require a business or government entity to notify an individual when there is a reasonable basis to conclude that a hacker or other criminal has obtained unencrypted personal data maintained by the entity;

- Define as personal data an individual's Social Security number, driver's license number, state identification number, bank account number, or credit card number;

- Subject entities that fail to comply with fines by the Federal Trade Commission of $5,000 per violation or up to $25,000 per day while the violation persists (State Attorneys General can also file suit to enforce the statute); and

- Allow California's new law to remain in effect, but preempt conflicting state laws, so as not to put companies in a situation that forces them to comply with database notification laws of 50 different states.

The legislation's notification scheme minimizes the burdens on companies or agencies that must report a database breach, and in general, notice would have to be provided to each person whose data was compromised in writing or through e-mail. But there are important exceptions:

- Companies that have developed their own reasonable notification policies are given a safe harbor under the bill and are exempted from its notification requirements;

- Encrypted data is exempted; and

- Where it is too expensive or impractical (e.g, contact address information is incomplete) to notify every individual who is harmed, the bill allows entities to send out an alternative form of notice called "substitute notice." Substitute notice includes posting notice on a website or notifying major media.

Substitute notice would be triggered if any of the following factors exist:

(i) the agency or person demonstrates that the cost of providing direct notice would exceed $250,000;

(ii) the affected class of subject persons to be notified exceeds 500,000; or

(iii) the agency or person does not have sufficient contact information to notify people whose information is at risk.

###

PRIVACY TIMES

EDITOR: EVAN HENDRICKS

Testimony of

Evan Hendricks, Editor/Publisher
Privacy Times
www.privacytimes.com

Before The Senate Committee On The Judiciary
Subcommittee On Terrorism, Technology & Homeland Security
November 4, 2003
Hearing: "Database Security: Finding Out When Your Information Has Been Compromised"

Mr. Chairman, Ranking Member Senator Feinstein, thank you for the opportunity to testify before the Subcommittees. My name is Evan Hendricks, Editor & Publisher of Privacy Times, a Washington newsletter since 1981. For the past 26 years, I have studied, reported on and published on a wide range of privacy issues, including credit, medical, employment, Internet, communications and government records. I have authored books about privacy and the Freedom of Information Act. I have served as an expert witness in litigation, and as an expert consultant for government agencies and corporations.

I want to commend the Chairman for holding this hearing, and commend Senator Feinstein for her leadership in introducing S 1350, "Notification of Risk To Personal Data Act." In an April 3 House Banking Subcommittee hearing that focused on three troubling examples of massive database security breaches, I recommended that Congress use the California State Law on notification as the starting point for enacting a national standard for all Americans. S 1350 is an important step toward achieving this worthy goal.

Privacy Times, Inc. P.O. Box 302 Cabin John, MD 20818 (301) 229 7002
(301) 229 8011 [Fax] evan@privacytimes.com

<u>Defining Privacy: "Fair Information Practices"</u>

When it comes to the collection, use and disclosure of personal information, privacy in our modern age is defined by principles known as Fair Information Practices (FIPs). This definition is recognized and accepted by nearly all Western Governments, including the U.S. Government, by academic and legal experts, and by such international bodies as the Organization of Economic Cooperation and Development (OECD), the European Union and the United Nations.

The principles are the foundation for the Fair Credit Reporting Act, the Privacy Act and several other information-privacy laws. As articulated by the OECD in 1980, they cover such issues as access and correction, transparency, data security, specifying and limiting the purposes for which data can be used, data minimization, and enforcement. In the mid-1990s, when the Federal Trade Commission took the lead for establishing the U.S. Government's privacy policy on electronic commerce, it distilled the FIPs into five principles: (1) Notice; (2) Choice/Consent; (3) Access; (4) Security and (5) Enforcement.

A fundamental premise of FIPs is that they create <u>rights</u> for individual and <u>duties</u> for organizations that collect and maintain personal data.

S 1350 is an excellent starting point because it recognizes two important principles. First, that transparency – more "sunshine" on organizational data practices – is imperative if personal privacy is to be protected. Second, that data security is vital to safeguarding privacy and that if security is breached, the individual has a right to know.

The legislation is the latest in a 30-year trend to convince companies to be more proactive about data security. The U.S. Privacy Act of 1974 requires Federal Agencies to "establish appropriate administrative, technical and physical safeguards to insure" security and confidentiality and "protect against anticipated threats . . . which could result in substantial harm, embarrassment, inconvenience or unfairness to any individual."

Under several federal court rulings regarding the FCRA, companies are vicariously liable for employees who pull credit reports for unauthorized purposes. As the U.S. Court of Appeals for the Sixth Circuit pointed out in its 1998 opinion in <u>Jones v. Federal Fin. Reserve Corp.</u> (144 3d 961), "Protecting consumers from the improper use of credit reports in an underlying policy of the FCRA. An apparent authority theory is in keeping with FCRA's underlying deterrent purpose because employers are in a better position to protect consumers by use of internal safeguards." In Kodrick v. Ferguson (54 F.Supp.2d 788), U.S. District Judge Moran wrote that sloppy security practices "almost invite violations" of credit report privacy.

The Gramm-Leach Bliley Act imposes data security duties on financial institutions. Moreover, a Federal Trade Commission enforcement action made it clear that companies are subject to Section 5 "Unfair and Deceptive Practices" investigations if they claim to observe security as part of their privacy policies but then allow data leakages through sloppy practices. New York Attorney General Eliot Spitzer applied the State's unfair practices law in a recent enforcement action against Victoria's Secret for data leakages at its Web site.

Stronger requirements are needed because the threat to data security will continue to escalate for at least a few reasons.

First, identity theft continues as one of the fastest growing crimes in the United States. In past months, new studies by the FTC, General Accounting Office, Gartner Group, Privacy & American Business and the Identity Theft Resource Center all found that the prevalence of identity theft, and the damage it causes, is far worse than previously believed. Increasingly, identity thieves are targeting organizational record systems in order to harvest the personal data necessary to engage in this form of fraud. In other words, our personal data has value and in the wrong hands, can be converted into near-instant credit. Moreover, the biggest threat to data security traditionally is posed by authorized insiders who decide to use personal information for unauthorized purposes. Fraud rings are known to bribe insiders in order to obtain personal data. This means that a person's privacy can be seriously jeopardized, but never learn about it, or learn well after even more damage has been done.

Second, there is a community of hackers constantly probing and testing data security. We still do not know the percentage of hackers that are hacking for malicious purposes. However, we do know that there is a community of "Carders," that is, hackers who specialize in obtaining and trafficking in credit card numbers. Hackers recently snared an unknown number of e-mail addresses from the Orbitz Web site, and then sent spam to those e-mail addresses. The FBI is investigating. It's not clear if Orbitz has notified all affected customers.

Third, despite the trend towards stronger legal duties cited above, there is not a strong organizational culture of data security throughout many organizations, even though they maintain or have access to the personal data of millions of Americans. This is due in part to the relative "newness" of the electronic data age, but in my opinion, more attributable to the absence of long-standing and well-known law and policy that would require organizations to take seriously the issues of data security and privacy.

New York AG Spitzer's investigation of Victoria's Secret was a case in point. Despite a succession of highly publicized data leakages causing harm to consumers and embarrassment and costs to companies, the company's Web site allowed anyone to access hundreds of customer names, addresses and orders through simple manipulation of the online customer identification number. The customer, Jason Sudowski, talked to a Victoria's Secret representative, but was told, "Well, there's no credit card numbers being displayed, so what's the big deal?" It was only after Sudowski called the media that the retailer fixed the glitch. And, it was only because of Spitzer's investigation that New York customers were notified and offered a remedy.

Another concern is the trend towards outsourcing data processing chores to overseas firms in lower-wage countries, including The Philippines, India, Pakistan and Jamaica. Equifax, the giant credit reporting agency (CRA), outsources some dispute handling to Jamaica. *Privacy Times* reported in September that the other two CRAs, Experian and Trans Union, were ready to begin outsourcing to The Philippines and India. A story in the Oct. 22 *San Francisco Chronicle* underscored one reason why this will increase security risks: A Pakistani employee of a subcontractor doing medical transcription for the Univ. of San Francisco Hospital, complained that the subcontractor had not paid for her work and threatened to post patient records on the Internet unless she was paid. The article noted that there are no enforceable privacy laws in Pakistan or the other low-wage countries to which personal data chores are being outsourced. It was this kind of scenario – the prospect of a citizen's data being exported to a country with inadequate law – that prompted the European Union to include trans border data flow restrictions in its directive on data protection.

HR 1350

Due to the relative suddenness of this hearing, I have not had the opportunity to fully analyze and contemplate all aspects of HR 1350. As I said, it is an excellent starting point. Here are some initial ways that the proposal could be improved:

Provide A Right Of Access. In order to be able to assess potential threats to their privacy, individuals need to know what information is being kept about them. The problem today is that in too many instances, Americans do not know what data are being kept on them – and don't even have a right to find out. A right of access will promote better security because organizations will need to authenticate individuals seeking access to their records. Individuals will be able to discover what information is being kept on them and, in some cases, opt out from systems, thereby removing their personal data and the threat altogether. Another benefit of access is the ability to correct inaccurate data, thereby promoting data integrity throughout the system. As Americans, we enjoy a right of access to our credit reports under FCRA, our federal records under the Privacy Act and Freedom of Information Act, our State records under State FOIA/PA laws, our medical records under HIPAA, our Cable TV records under the 1984 Cable TV law, and to a lesser extent, insurance and employment records under various State laws. We need to extend access rights by law to personal data held by all major organizations. Further, in the electronic environment the cost and burden of providing access is decreasing.

Because notification of consumers should only be required when a breach or leakage has the potential for harm, there will be cases in which a more routine breach will not result in notification. In such cases, it is imperative that individuals have the right to learn 1) if the organization maintains data on them; and 2) what procedures the organization has to protect data and provide notice in significant cases. Again, this fits squarely into the category of "Sunshine being the best disinfectant."

Adopt The Privacy Act's Security Standard. As mentioned above, Section (e)(10) of the Privacy Act requires Federal agencies to "establish appropriate administrative, technical and physical safeguards to insure" security and confidentiality and "protect against anticipated threats . . . which could result in substantial harm, embarrassment, inconvenience or unfairness to any individual." Federal agencies have lived under this standard without much problem. In fact, a similar standard is likely to evolve for financial institutions due to regulations proposed by banking agencies under GLB. This standard should be extended to all major organizations that handle sensitive personal data.

Create A Private Right of Action. S 1350 logically delegates enforcement to the FTC and State AGs, the entities that have been most active in enforcing privacy and consumer protection laws. However, the bill also needs a private right of action so that individuals can go to court to enforce their own rights. Remember we are talking about mammoth databases maintaining records on anywhere between a few million to 210 million Americans. Given this scope, you will never be able – nor would you want—to build a bureaucracy large enough to carry out adequate enforcement. The private right of action needs to include minimum statutory damages, attorney's fees and injunctive relief. This right would only apply to serious cases where the company's conduct was determined to be "gross negligence" or a "reckless disregard for the rights of consumers."

Curtail The Use of SSNs as a personal identifier. The SSN is the first tool of choice of identity thieves. Restricting the circulation of SSNs by restricting their use outside of government, employment and banking, will reduce risks. Sen. Feinstein, Sen. Bunning, Rep. Clay Shaw, and others have introduced legislative proposals to this effect.

Create An Independent Privacy Office. Most people don't realize that Sen. Sam Ervin originally proposed such an office along with the Privacy Act. Now, every advanced nation has one except the United States.

Thank you for this opportunity to testify. I would be happy to answer any questions.

STATEMENT OF SENATOR JON KYL
CHAIRMAN
SUBCOMMITTEE ON TERRORISM, TECHNOLOGY, AND HOMELAND SECURITY
SENATE JUDICIARY COMMITTEE
4 NOVEMBER 2003

Introduction

The theft by a computer hacker of a person's Social Security number, driver's license, or financial information can be devastating. A criminal can use this information to cause great financial harm.

S. 1350

Senator Feinstein's bill, S. 1350, the "Notification of Risk to Personal Data Act," addresses the duty of a business maintaining a computerized database with customers' sensitive personal information to inform customers of a hacking incident that compromises personal financial data.

Under the bill, notice would be triggered if the hacker obtained access to a customer's (1) Social Security number, (2) driver license number, or (3) bank account, debit, or credit card number.

Notice would be provided to individuals (1) in writing, (2) through e-mail, or (3) by substitute notice. Substitute notice can be used to prevent undue burdens on agencies or companies. Substitute notice includes notice by e-mail, the posting of notice on the company, or agency website or the notification of major media. Substitute notice is triggered if any of the following factors exist:

(i) the business demonstrates that the cost of providing direct notice would exceed $250,000;

(ii) the business of subject persons to be notified exceeds 500,000; or

(iii) the business does not have sufficient contact information to notify people whose information is at risk.

Finally, under the bill, the Federal Trade Commission is empowered to fine entities $5,000 per violation or up to $25,000 per day while the violation persists. State Attorneys General can enforce the statute. Inconsistent state laws are preempted, but California's legislation is grandfathered-in.

Witnesses

Today, the Technology subcommittee will hear from three expert witnesses:

- The first witness is from my home state of Arizona. David McIntyre is the President and CEO of TriWest Healthcare Alliance. Mr. McIntyre has a distinguished career in both health care policy and operations. Earlier this year, he guided TriWest in its successful bid for the Defense Department's new West Region, serving military members, retirees, and their families in 21 Western states — including our ranking Member's state of California — a total of 2.6 million beneficiaries in all.

  Mr. McIntyre will testify about the December 2002 break-in at its Phoenix, Arizona offices. Thieves broke into a management suite and stole laptop computers and computer hard drives containing the names, address, telephone numbers, birth dates, and Social Security numbers of 562,000 military service members, dependents, and retirees. The thieves also stole medical claims records for people on active duty in the Persian Gulf. The potential harm to a group this large, particularly to those who wear the uniform of this country, was staggering. Yet, to date, not a single individual has suffered identity theft as a result of the crime against TriWest.

  Mr. McIntyre, we look forward to your description of those events and how your company responded to such a major information theft.

- Mark MacCarthy, the Senior Vice President of Public Policy for Visa will testify about the steps that VISA takes to avoid database security breaches and how VISA notifies its customers of any security breech. He will also comment on S.1350.

- Evan Hendricks, Editor, Privacy Times, will testify about the rise of database security breaches, the types of information stolen from databases, the failure to notify consumers of such breaches, and the value of notification.

Closing

In closing, I would like to note that the record will be kept open for one week for questions and for additional statements.

I would like to thank Senator Feinstein for her hard work in putting together this hearing. On this issue and every issue before the subcommittee she has worked diligently and has been a great pleasure to work with.

#

U.S. SENATOR PATRICK LEAHY

CONTACT: David Carle, 202-224-3693 VERMONT

Statement of Senator Patrick Leahy,
Ranking Member, Senate Judiciary Committee
Hearing On
"Database Security:
Finding Out When Your Information Has Been Compromised"
November 4, 2003

Today's hearing will examine the timely and important issues related to database security. As technology has advanced, and particularly since the terrorist attacks of September 11th, there has been a surge in government and private sector efforts to create large databases that compile extensive personal information, often through so-called data-mining. The Bush Administration has done this in the name of homeland security, and private companies have argued that gathering this information is essential to their commercial ventures.

We are well aware of the concerns that these databases can foster and the problems that can result from their misuse. Administration projects like the Total Information Awareness initiative threatened to violate privacy and other civil liberties and provoked an overwhelming outcry from the public. Just recently we learned that a DOD contractor, Torch Concepts, obtained an airline passenger database without those passengers' knowledge, used it in ways not admitted to the airline, and publicly released the personal information of one of those unsuspecting passengers.

I am particularly concerned that criminals view these databases as virtual goldmines for illegal activities, most notably identity theft. I commend Senator Feinstein for introducing S.1350 to alleviate some of the concerns with these personal information databases. I also commend her steady and committed leadership on identity theft.

Since the 104th Congress, I have worked on many efforts to protect consumers against identity theft. I collaborated with Senators Grassley and Kyl on the National Information Infrastructure Protection Act of 1996, to protect financial and other data from threats directed against computers and computer systems. Senator Kyl and I also cosponsored the Identity Theft and Assumption Deterrence Act of 1998, signed into law by President Clinton, to penalize the theft of personal identification information for false credit cards, fraudulent loans or for other illegal purposes.

In the 106th Congress, I supported the Internet False Identification Prevention Act, also signed into law by President Clinton, to provide additional tools to law enforcement to combat the theft of, and fraud associated with, identification documents and credentials.

senator_leahy@leahy.senate.gov
http://leahy.senate.gov/

I also joined Senators Grassley and Breaux in introducing S.1723, the Protect Victims of Identity Theft Act of 2001, to clarify that the statute of limitations for identity theft does not start until the consumer discovers the problem or should have discovered it through the exercise of reasonable diligence. I also cosponsored a substitute to S.1742, the Identity Theft Victims Assistance Act, to assist identity theft victims restore their credit ratings and reclaim their good names by giving them the right to obtain relevant business records and the ability to have fraudulent charges blocked from reporting in their consumer credit reports.

This year I have cosponsored S. 223, which, among other steps, would set procedural guidelines for consumer reporting agencies to notify consumers about address discrepancies in their files, prohibit printing the last five digits of credit card numbers and expiration dates on receipts, and require that consumer reporting agencies provide consumers with one free annual credit report. I have also cosponsored S.228, which would criminalize the display, sale or purchase of social security numbers without individual consent, prohibit the display of social security numbers on certain public documents, like driver's licenses and government checks, and prohibit companies from requiring consumers to provide social security numbers when buying goods or services.

Unless we are vigilant about protecting them, our privacy rights can easily slip away through erosion. I have long encouraged diligence in our Committee's role in defending privacy rights. I welcome today's hearing, I welcome our witnesses today, and I look forward to learning more about their efforts to ensure database security and prevent identity theft.

#####

WRITTEN STATEMENT

OF

MARK MACCARTHY

ON BEHALF OF

VISA U.S.A. INC.

BEFORE THE

SUBCOMMITTEE ON

TERRORISM, TECHNOLOGY AND HOMELAND SECURITY

OF THE

COMMITTEE ON THE JUDICIARY

UNITED STATES SENATE

November 4, 2003

Mr. Chairman, Ranking Member Feinstein and Members of the Subcommittee, my name is Mark MacCarthy. I am Senior Vice President for Public Policy for Visa U.S.A. Inc. Thank you for the invitation to participate in this hearing. Visa appreciates the opportunity to address the important issues raised by S. 1350, the "Notification of Risk to Personal Data Act" ("S. 1350"). S. 1350 would require federal agencies and persons engaged in interstate commerce, that own or license electronic data containing personal information, to notify affected individuals of any unauthorized acquisition of such information.

The Visa Payment System, of which Visa U.S.A.[1] is a part, is the largest consumer payment system, and the leading consumer e-commerce payment system, in the world, with more volume than all other major payment cards combined. Visa plays a pivotal role in advancing new payment products and technologies, including technology initiatives for protecting personal information and preventing identity theft and other fraud, for the benefit of its member financial institutions and their hundreds of millions of cardholders.

Visa commends the Subcommittee for focusing on the important issue of consumer information security. As the leading consumer electronic commerce payment system in the world, Visa considers it a top priority to remain a leader in the development of technology, products, and services that protect consumers from the effects of information security breaches. As a result, Visa has long recognized the importance of strict internal procedures to protect the customer information of Visa's members, thereby protecting the integrity of the Visa system. Visa is currently implementing a comprehensive and aggressive customer information security program known as the Cardholder Information Security Plan ("CISP"). This security program applies to all entities that store, process, transmit, or hold Visa cardholder data. CISP was developed, and is already being used, to ensure that the customer information of Visa's members is kept protected and confidential. Additionally, as a part of CISP, Visa requires that all

---

[1] Visa U.S.A. is a membership organization comprised of U.S. financial institutions licensed to use the Visa service marks in connection with payment systems.

participating entities comply with the "Visa Digital Dozen"—twelve basic requirements for safeguarding accounts. These include: (1) install and maintain a working network firewall to protect data; (2) keep security patches up-to-date; (3) protect stored data; (4) encrypt data sent across public networks; (5) use and regularly update anti-virus software; (6) restrict access to data by "need-to-know;" (7) assign a unique ID to each person with computer access; (8) do not use vendor-supplied defaults for system passwords and security parameters; (9) track all access to data by unique ID; (10) regularly test security systems and processes; (11) implement and maintain an overall information security policy; and (12) restrict physical access to data.

In addition, Visa's information security policy for the treatment of personal information includes sophisticated neural networks that flag unusual spending patterns for fraud and block the authorization of transactions where fraud is suspected. As an additional customer protection, the Visa system provides for zero liability for unauthorized customer transactions, thereby significantly limiting the potential harm to Visa cardholders from information security breaches, including identity theft. Visa also maintains the Exception File, a worldwide database of account numbers of lost/stolen cards or other cards that issuers have designated for confiscation, referral to issuers, or other special handling. All transactions routed through the Visa Payment System have their account numbers checked against the Exception File.

Visa believes that the appropriate response to a security breach affecting customer information depends on the specific factors of that breach, including the information accessed, the extent to which the interloper who accessed the information has had an opportunity to use or further disclose the information for illicit purposes, and the tools available to both the financial institution and its customers to identify and address the illicit use of customer information. In addition, an appropriate response must balance the risks of illicit use of the information affected, against the risks that the response itself may lead to customer cost and inconvenience that are actually greater than the risk of illicit use of the information under the circumstances.

The latter issue has particular significance when determining whether customer notification is appropriate following any particular security breach. Critical to the concept of customer notification is the idea that a customer receiving that notification can take steps to protect him or herself against identity theft or other fraud. Customer scrutiny of billing statements for unauthorized transactions, the ability to close fraudulently established accounts, the ability of customers to place fraud alerts on their files at consumer reporting agencies, and the ability of customers to review their consumer reporting agency files are all important steps in preventing identity theft and other fraud.

However, in the context of payment card accounts—both credit card and debit card accounts—these steps serve merely as backstops to the far more sophisticated fraud detection systems currently in place for both existing and new accounts, including the Visa cardholder account fraud detection systems and the customer identification requirements mandated by Section 326 of the USA PATRIOT Act. Moreover, while scrutiny of billing statements should be routine, the closing of accounts, the placing of fraud alerts, and the review of files at consumer reporting agencies involve costs and inconvenience for both the customer and the marketplace as a whole. For example, closed accounts must be replaced, fraud alerts may impede future transactions, and repeated access to consumer reporting agency files is costly. Moreover, a proliferation of fraud alerts that are not related to actual fraud can dilute the effectiveness of fraud alert programs, since a series of false positives makes it more difficult to identify real fraud, potentially making identity theft easier rather than harder.

Given these considerations, Visa believes that an appropriate response to a security breach should involve a three-step process. First, an assessment of the fraud risks associated with the particular breach, second, an assessment of the tools available to address those risks, and third, an assessment of whether and the extent to which customer participation is likely to be an important element of controlling those risks; in other words, the utilization of a risk-based model for customer notification.

Accordingly, Visa strongly supports customer notification whenever unauthorized access to customer information results in a significant, recognizable threat that requires customer action. However, for situations that involve unauthorized access to customer information, but which do not indicate a significant risk that customer information will be the subject of fraud or misuse, notification of customers is not necessary.

In the context of the Visa system, Visa believes that notification of a security breach should only be undertaken when there is clear evidence that the information that has been the subject of a security breach is being used for fraudulent purposes. Further, Visa believes that it is critical that any notification requirements be sufficiently flexible to allow notice to be provided by the account holding institution whose customer is affected by the security breach where the account holding institution believes that it can minimize the disruptive effects of the notice, even if the account holding institution was not the operator of the system experiencing the breach. For example, the account holding institution may wish to offer a new account at the same time that it advises the customer that it may be necessary to close his or her existing account.

Visa is pleased to note that S. 1350 is responsive to both of these issues. S. 1350 permits the use of alternative, reasonable notification procedures where those procedures include a security program, such as the Visa program, that is reasonably designed to block unauthorized transactions before they are charged to the customer's account, and which is subject to examination for compliance by one or more of the functional regulators identified in Section 509 of the Gramm-Leach-Bliley Act, including the federal banking agencies. S. 1350 also provides for flexibility in delivering any required notice in order to minimize the disruptions to existing relationships.

Finally, Visa also is pleased to note that S. 1350 recognizes the importance of establishing consistent procedures for notifying individuals about security breaches and supersedes inconsistent state and local laws.

Visa appreciates the opportunity to appear before you today. We believe our information security response program creates a comfortable and secure environment for consumers engaged in financial transactions. Combating information security breaches and identity theft will continue as a top priority of Visa and its member financial institutions.

I would be happy to answer any questions that you may have.

TRIWEST HEALTHCARE ALLIANCE

Written Testimony of

David J. McIntyre, Jr.
President and CEO
TriWest Healthcare Alliance

Before the

U.S. Senate Judiciary Committee,
Subcommittee on Terrorism, Technology
and Homeland Security

November 4, 2003

Introduction

Chairman Kyl, Senator Feinstein and distinguished members of the Judiciary Committee, Subcommittee on Terrorism, Technology and Homeland Security. I would like to thank you for the invitation to appear before you today to discuss the important topic of identity theft. Unfortunately, this has become an increasingly prevalent issue and as consumers we are all concerned. I would like to thank you for the focus you are giving this critical issue and for your desire to enhance safeguards for consumers. In fact, a number of you have been involved in this issue for some time.

My name is David McIntyre. I am the president and CEO of TriWest Healthcare Alliance, a private corporation that administers the Department of Defense's (DoD's) TRICARE program in the 16-state Central Region and will soon do so across the expanded 21 state area known as the TRICARE West Region with the recent award of a 5 year - $10 billion contract that adds the states of California, Oregon, Washington, Alaska and Hawaii to those who already serve. We are the largest government contractor based in the state of Arizona, with soon to be substantial operations in California and these other states. The company I lead is privileged to serve the health care needs of those who have or currently defend our freedom and their families.

In mid-December, our company was the victim of a theft that placed at risk the personal information of more than a half-million current and former TriWest customers (TRICARE beneficiaries), many of whom are also our employees.

As you know, identity theft is a serious federal crime that affects more and more Americans each year. This crime causes billions of dollars of harm to Americans each year. The thieves who commit these crimes against consumers don't just acquire merchandise illegally or use fake identification to obtain anything from a driver's license to a job; they wreak havoc on the lives of their victims. Repairing the damage done to a victim's credit record is costly and time-consuming. In fact, it often takes years for a victim of identity theft to clear up the mess created, and sometimes, their credit is permanently ruined.

In my opinion, there are few consumer issues more worthy of the attention of your Committee than this topic. And, on behalf of TriWest's employees and those we serve, I would like to commend you for your focus on this rapidly growing crime and the importance you are placing on the need for action. I am hopeful that your efforts will be successful and that they serve to enhance protection for America's consumers from this insidious crime. Accordingly, I am pleased to be here today to share the details of our story and to encourage you to take action to protect consumers.

I am particularly honored today to be in the presence of my home state Senator, Jon Kyl, and Senator Diane Feinstein, both of whom have been important leaders in the effort to combat identity theft. I applaud your leadership on this critical consumer issue and thank you for the invitation to appear before you today.

TriWest Healthcare Alliance and the TRICARE Central Region Beneficiaries

TriWest is the Managed Care Support Contractor for the current 16-state TRICARE Central Region. We partner with the military to meet the health care needs of more than 1.1 million members of our nation's military family (active duty, their families, and retirees and their family members). And, as I stated, we are in the process of transition into five additional states – California, Oregon, Washington, Alaska and Hawaii. This territory includes 48% of the land mass of the United States, where we will provide services for some 2.6 million members of our nation's military family.

Based in Phoenix, Arizona, we have remote office locations across the 16-state Central Region. Most of our offices are on military installations.

TRICARE Central Region

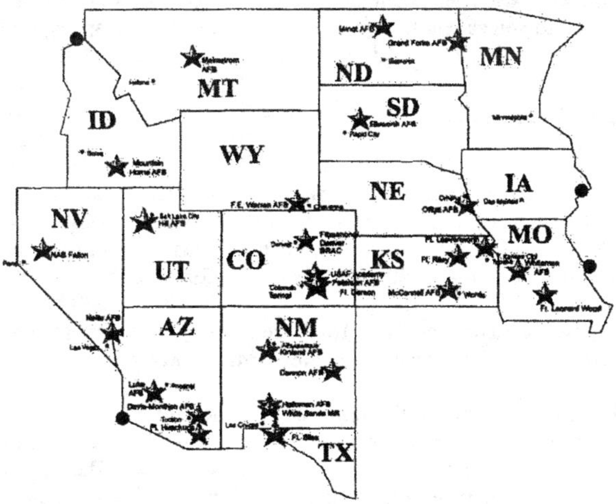

● Areas not included in the TRICARE Central Region: Yuma, Ariz., contained in Region 10; six northern counties in Idaho contained in Region 11; certain ZIP codes in the St. Louis, Mo. area, and the Rock Island Arsenal area in Iowa, contained in Region 5.

TriWest has a strong history of collaboration and partnering with our military/ government counterparts in the Central Region. In addition, we remain steadfastly amenable to providing information to the DoD, Congress, and Committees such as these, to the benefit of the TRICARE program overall, as well as the deserving population we serve.

As I have come to learn since December of last year, identity theft is the No. 1 consumer fraud in the nation. Nearly one million Americans were victimized last year alone. California ranks first in the country when it comes to the state with the greatest prevalence of identity theft; and Arizona ranks second. Given the impact on Americans who become the victims of these crimes, I believe this is an issue that demands action.

Due to the theft perpetrated against our corporation in mid-December, I have come to learn firsthand about identity theft. As a consumer, I now know the importance of keeping tabs on my credit files and billing statements in an effort to safeguard my personal information. As a business leader, I have learned that it is absolutely critical for companies to be more aggressive about security in all aspects of their operation.

Because TriWest is committed to providing exemplary service to those who sacrifice so much on our behalf, our Board of Directors, leadership team and staff at TriWest take a personal interest in matters that affect our customers. I am honored to be with you today to share what happened to us in mid-December, how we responded to the theft, and the invaluable lessons we have learned about identity theft. I hope that our sharing this information is helpful to you as you seek to determine what policy changes need to be made to provide optimal protection to America's consumers again this terrible crime.

Computer Theft at TriWest's Secondary Corporate Office

On Saturday morning, December 14, our secondary corporate office in Phoenix, AZ, was burglarized. Computer equipment and data files containing confidential and personal files of more than 500,000 members of America's military family were stolen from the premises. The information included on the stolen hard drives includes names, addresses and Social Security numbers, along with other personal information.

The burglary was discovered on December 16. Since that day, TriWest has coordinated closely with the authorities who are conducting the criminal investigation.

The identity of those who committed this crime and the motives behind the crime remain unknown. While information has been compromised, we do not have any verification that anyone's personal information has been misused or will be misused. The very possibility, however, that it could have been misused called for prompt action on our part to inform our customers about the compromising of their personal information and education about the steps they can take to protect themselves.

Health care professionals talk about the "Golden Hour" when they refer to the window in which it is critical that heart attack victims receive medical attention if they are to have high odds for survival and a reasonable quality of life. What I quickly discovered is that there is a "Golden Hour" when it comes to aiding consumers in protecting themselves against identity theft as well. The experts told me that if it we wanted the best chance of protecting our customers from identity theft, we had no more than a couple of weeks to reach our customers and assist them in contacting the credit bureaus so they could act to place fraud flags on the credit files. In a case like this, a few weeks is the amount of time thieves would need to take the database and make credit instruments to perpetrate identity theft. Like the critical care needed for the heart attack victim, notifying our beneficiaries was the most effective course and it had to be done quickly.

It was this "golden hour" philosophy that guided our work and that of the Department of Defense in the days and weeks following the theft.

Coordinated DoD/TriWest Response to the Theft

From the day we discovered the theft, we began coordinating with our DoD partners. Once we had compiled the list of affected individuals from our backup tapes, we began working around the clock with the leadership of the DoD and the Military Health System to create and implement an integrated comprehensive communication plan.

The plan employed a three-prong approach that began with TriWest contacting the media to broadcast the theft and stress the need for individuals to protect themselves. Second, the DoD, working through the military commands, disseminated information to every installation, worldwide. The third component of the communication plan included a letter campaign that contacted every beneficiary affected by the theft, and which included information on steps they could take to protect themselves against misuse of their personal information.

Within weeks, the timeframe of the "golden hour" defined for us by the experts, the execution of this communication plan was complete.

I would like to share with you, in detail, the specifics of our efforts; however, I would like to first express my deep personal gratitude to the DoD for responding to this issue, and to Dr. Bill Winkenwerder, the Assistant Secretary of Defense for Health Affairs, for the immediate personal attention he gave the theft and the invaluable leadership he provided as we worked side-by-side with the other leaders throughout the Military Health System to deal with the situation. Without this coordinated response, our efforts to inform those impacted by the theft would not have been as successful.

This issue was a critical focus for our company. First and foremost, we believed it was necessary to alert the DoD, as well as the affected individuals, so that they could take action to protect themselves, should the thieves choose to misuse the personal information they illegally obtained. The following is a detailed account of the activities we were engaged in as a result of the theft. These include our ongoing efforts and reflect our continued commitment to respond quickly and aggressively to this issue:

- Authorities were contacted; federal investigators worked to find the individual(s) responsible for the crime.

- TMA and SAIC personnel analyzed what, if any, additional security measures should be taken to protect TriWest from another theft.
- The DoD began working with TriWest to ensure an uninterrupted delivery of medical benefits.
- I personally called the 23 beneficiaries whose credit card information was stolen. Information regarding the theft was conveyed, and the beneficiaries were encouraged to take action to protect themselves from the misuse of their credit card. The beneficiaries were also provided contact information in the event they encounter any suspicious activity with their credit card.
- TriWest's proposed communication plan and messages were delivered to the Office of the Secretary of Defense (OSD) for review.
- All affected customers were contacted by mail to inform them of the theft and what the steps they needed to take to protect themselves from the possibility of "identity theft". Due to the fact that the credit bureaus are on different cycles for the update of fraud flags, with three months being the lowest common denominator, we have mailed our customers every quarter reminding them to update their fraud flag so that they will remain protected.
- A memo was distributed to all TriWest employees via email. Additional security policies were also distributed to all employees.
- The strategy for communicating the issue to beneficiaries was completed (with OSD approval).
- Ongoing communication updates were provided to TriWest's Board of Directors and subcontractors.
- Designated TriWest customer service personnel were trained to staff dedicated phone lines for incoming beneficiary calls.
- TriWest communicated with key Congressional leadership, Beneficiary Associations, and affected providers.
- Dr. Jerry Sanders, TriWest's Vice President of Medical Affairs and retired Deputy Surgeon General of the Air Force, personally contacted active and retired General Officers to inform them of the theft and our communication plan.

The communication strategy continued to be implemented throughout the holidays. By the end of December, TriWest had contacted each of the potentially affected individuals or families, and had also built a unique e-mail system, a web site and a call center to provide information and answer questions beneficiaries may have about the identity theft issue as well as the safeguards they can take to protect themselves. In addition, TriWest coordinated with the three credit bureaus to provide information on how to combat identity theft and place fraud alerts in their individual credit files.

Since the discovery of the theft, we at TriWest have taken measures to reconfigure our systems and enhance our security. In addition, we worked with federal personnel and a top private sector information security company to review all aspects of our physical and data security in an attempt to make sure that we understood all of the actions we should take to minimize the chance that such an event is repeated and we have taken those actions.

As a result of the break-in at our secondary corporate facility, we have learned a great deal about the issue of identity theft; it quickly became apparent to us how difficult it can be to catch those who commit such crimes. And, as it turned out, we were one of several health care and financial organizations in Arizona over a six month period that had been burglarized only to have the hard drives containing databases with personal consumer information stolen from their computers. In an effort to assist local and federal law enforcement in their pursuit of who was responsible for this crime, we posted the largest reward of its kind in the history of Arizona -- $100,000 for anyone who brought forward information leading to the arrest and successful prosecution of those responsible for this very serious federal crime -- a crime affecting more than 500,000 of our nation's patriots. My Board and I had been hopeful that this $100,000 reward that we posted would encourage anyone that might know something to come forward and inform the authorities about the people responsible for this crime and the location of the stolen information. Unfortunately, that has not been the case.

The good news is that, to date, as far as we and the authorities are able to tell, no one's personal information has been misused as a result of the theft of our computer equipment and files.

Invaluable Lessons Learned

The theft of this computer equipment and the files contained within was and remains a matter of grave concern to everyone at TriWest as well as the DoD. As a result of the theft, and because it was the right thing to do, we became a more security-conscious organization.

We conducted a thorough security vulnerability assessment, took action to improve security across the enterprise, and, while I am not sure an organization can ever be fully immune to the risk of such thefts, we are confident we have contained further significant threats to our beneficiaries' personal information.

However, we will never become complacent with respect to maintaining the privacy of our beneficiaries.

The following are some of the steps we have taken to make sure nothing similar to this event ever happens within our organization again.

- TriWest has built an information technology infrastructure that includes enhanced security features.
- TriWest established a Security Steering Group with responsibilities to oversee data and physical security policies and practices throughout our corporation. The Security Steering Group reports directly to me as President and CEO. Specific duties of the Group include:
    - Oversight of the IT security management program;
    - Oversight of the execution of the company's Facility Security Plan; and

    - o Human Resources actions to include access privileges, background checks, and other classification actions including security awareness training for all personnel.
- TriWest has upgraded its incident reporting system.
- TriWest has received initial authority as part of the DoD's DITSCAP requirements (the DoD's security certification and accreditation process) and exceeded some implementation requirements by employing state-of-the-art security procedures.

<u>Protecting Our Customers from Identity Theft</u>

While we clearly suffered a burglary, and that was a significant concern, my greatest concern was what steps we could take to protect our customers from having the people who stole this equipment and the databases it contained from committing crimes against them by misusing the information to perpetrate identity theft.

In taking action, we researched information published by the Social Security and Federal Trade Commission (FTC) relating to information and identity theft. We developed a white paper, "Safeguard Yourself," as well as a telephone call center script that was based on the information we'd gathered. The paper included a description of the process our beneficiaries should employ to determine whether they are a victim of information or identity theft; how to initiate the placement of a fraud alert on their credit records; and how to contact each of the three credit bureaus in the United States. We submitted the paper to the attorneys in the FTC department that oversees identity theft and requested their review and suggested edits. They were extremely cooperative and helpful in reviewing the information we planned to provide our beneficiaries.

Following the review of our paper, one of the FTC attorneys, Naomi Lefkovitz, provided us with suggested contact points at each of the credit bureaus. We called each one to advise them of our situation and to seek their assistance and advice. They reported that the calls related to our theft caused a 300–400% increase in calls to their call centers.

A review of the calls received by our own Theft Hotline indicated that beneficiaries were asking whether TriWest could initiate the fraud alert with the credit bureaus on their behalf. This issue was a point of discussion between TriWest and the DoD; and a determination was made by the DoD Privacy Officer that, with permission of the person involved, we could initiate the fraud alert on their behalf.

Hence, discussions were held with each of the credit bureaus. TransUnion and Equifax agreed to accept requests, consistent with Privacy Act requirements, from us on behalf of beneficiaries. TriWest developed a plan that allowed beneficiaries to complete a request and authorization form on our web site, which was then transmitted to the credit bureau for their action. This process was implemented in an encrypted, secure manner. Experian determined that they would establish a web-based request for Fraud Alerts and an online viewing of the consumer's credit report. It was their preference for the consumer to enter their request directly into Experian's system via a hotlink from TriWest's web site.

Each of the credit bureau representatives noted that this was the first arrangement of this nature by their organizations on behalf of consumers.

This process is still in place. Upon receipt of the request and identifying information, the credit bureaus send a letter of notification regarding the fraud alert to the beneficiary, along with a copy of their credit report. (These arrangements were all made at no cost to the individual beneficiary.) The web request for fraud alerts was activated at the end of January 2003; since that time, over 63,000 beneficiaries have initiated fraud alerts.

Development of the web process for fraud alert requests made the process much more convenient for beneficiaries. By accepting batches of data files rather than thousands of calls to their call centers, it also served as a means of cost avoidance for the credit bureaus' call center operating costs. The credit bureaus were exceptionally helpful and responsive throughout this entire process, on both the technical and executive levels. Their advice, assistance, and cooperation have been noteworthy and extremely valuable.

And, as you may know, they have gone even further. They now share information on a regular basis… all to make processes easier for the consumer.

Needed Congressional Action

Without a doubt, we must rein in identity theft. Again that is why I am so appreciative of the focus that this Committee is giving to this critical consumer issue. Companies and consumers must take more aggressive steps to combat this crime and protect themselves. Based on all I have learned about this topic, I believe Congress needs to take action in three areas.

First, I very strongly believe that any organizational leader, be it public or private, whose organization suffers the theft of customers' personal information has an absolute obligation to inform those customers of such an event and help them understand what they can do to protect themselves against the misuse of that information. I understand personally the difficulty, cost and awkward nature of such disclosure, but to do anything less is wrong and indefensible.

After all, we are merely stewards of our customers' personal information as we seek to serve their needs. This is not our information; it belongs to our customers. And to not inform them of such an event for fear that we would lose their confidence or subject our company to negative publicity is unacceptable. It places our customers at even greater risk by preventing them from taking steps to protect themselves.

The safeguards that consumers can take to shield themselves from fraudulent uses of their personal information are uncomplicated and, if accomplished quickly enough after the theft, quite effective. Quick and decisive actions such as flagging your credit file, notifying your bank and other major creditors to watch for unusual activity and contacting the Federal Trade Commission to file a complaint can save years of expensive and time-consuming effort for consumers affected by such thefts.

It is for this reason that I appreciate Senator Feinstein's work in drawing attention to the issue and proposing constructive solutions with S. 1350, the Notification of Risk to Personal Data Act.

While some may suggest that we ought to simply leave it to organizations and the marketplace, to define the proper response to these incidents and the consequences for not taking appropriate action, I would suggest that this is neither fair nor appropriate for the consumer.

The "golden hour" in this area has been defined, and the consequence to the individual consumer of an organization not taking appropriate measures to inform them that their personal information has been compromised so that they can take measures to protect themselves places them at risk of individual financial ruin. We now know the effective ways to deal with this threat, and the credit bureaus have worked hard to put effective measures in place to support the consumer. Thus, I do not believe it unreasonable to say to those of us who have been entrusted with consumer information to meet the needs of our customers that the known theft or release of such information into the public domain triggers a requirement to arm the effected consumers with the necessary information so that they can take measures to protect themselves.

Second, as a consumer, I've observed the inconsistencies in how credit card numbers/accounts are handled among merchants. Specifically, I have noticed the variance in how credit card numbers are displayed on receipts. For instance, some receipts include the entire credit card number, expiration date and full name of the cardholder, which means the card number can now be used by anyone who happens to pick up the receipt. Other receipt slips contain only the last four digits of the credit card number, which offers more protection against misuse of the account.

I believe that standardization of how credit card numbers are displayed on receipts, to block out most of the numbers, is one more way in which Americans could be better protected against identity theft, as it would help to minimize this type of criminal activity. I believe that the provisions contained in the legislation to reauthorize the Fair Credit Reporting Act, which I understand will be on the Senate floor for action soon, go a long way to address this issue and are worthy of your support.

And third, I believe the federal penalties for identity theft offer little deterrent to those bent on committing such a serious crime. For example, I was appalled to learn that the maximum federal penalty for such crimes is five years in prison and a $250,000 fine. These penalties must be significantly increased to serve both as an effective deterrent and a sufficient punishment. It is amazing to me that those who perpetrate such crimes often spend less time in jail than it takes the average consumer to clean up their credit. This has got to be fixed.

During the 107th Congress, lawmakers introduced more than two dozen bills to thwart identity theft and assist victims. Unfortunately, none of them made it into law.

I hope that the 108th Congress will be able to muster the support to move legislation in this area – strengthen the laws used to deal with those who perpetrate such crimes and enhance the protections for Americans.

Without question, the process of changing our laws is difficult. Our system of government requires careful deliberation, and that takes time. But thieves don't have to wait for public debate. They utilize new technologies as soon as they figure out how to profit from them. As a result, laws often play catch-up to technology. And, as our case and the others you will be hearing about today suggest, the criminals unfortunately have the upper hand.

Federal and state laws have yet to be tightened to provide law enforcement with effective enough tools to aggressively deal with the onslaught of identity theft. Unfortunately, in the breach lies the consumer. Identity thieves know that if they are caught, the current punishment is vastly inferior to, for example, robbing a bank. Yet, the impact of the crime is no less serious.

It is my hope that this Committee and Congress will be successful in championing the cause of strengthening the protections and penalties that predate the information age and take steps to modify the rules to add an effective layer of protection for all of us.

Conclusion

In an effort to protect our customers, we have dealt aggressively with this issue. We have communicated with all of the affected parties and the government. In addition, we have shared this experience and the lessons learned with all of the Department of Defense Health System's contractors and the direct care system.

The criminal investigation remains active, led by the Defense Criminal Investigative Service and supported by the U.S. Attorney in Phoenix, the Federal Bureau of Investigation, and other law enforcement agencies.

We have been commended for our response to the theft and our honesty in communicating with those whose personal information was put at risk. In fact, we have received many words of praise from our beneficiaries. Of note, Chairman Myers of the Joint Chiefs of Staff, a former beneficiary of ours, whose name was included in the stolen data files, sent us a letter to applaud us for our immediate and responsive actions to the situation. While we appreciate the praise, all we did was respond by doing what we thought was the right thing by our customers who were infringed upon and whose financial integrity was placed at risk due to the burglary we suffered.

TriWest Healthcare Alliance takes great pride in the work that we perform. It is a privilege and a pleasure to support the Military Health System and the beneficiaries of the current TRICARE Central Region and the soon to be TRICARE West Region. These are the very individuals currently putting their lives on the line for freedom.

I am grateful that your Committee and its members are focused on this very important topic. The commitment you have made to learn about the threat of identity theft and take a proactive stance against its rampant spread is not only admirable but is also the bridge that is needed to make the public more aware of the potential every American is susceptible to, while sending a message to the criminals who perpetrate such insidious crimes. I would like to thank you for the opportunity to share this experience with you and provide information to you on this critically important topic.

Thank you for the invitation to participate in today's hearing. I would be glad to answer any questions that you might have of me.

APEX
TP
9780160733079
76901945–84